science
museum

HOW TO BE A
BRAIN
SURGEON

Amanda Li

Illustrated by Mike Phillips

**MACMILLAN
CHILDREN'S BOOKS**

With grateful thanks to Will Cato-Addison and Nicky Cooper

First published 2006 by Macmillan Children's Books
a division of Macmillan Publishers Limited
20 New Wharf Road, London N1 9RR
Basingstoke and Oxford
www.panmacmillan.com

Associated companies throughout the world

ISBN-13: 978-0-330-44615-0
ISBN-10: 0-330-44615-0

Text copyright © Amanda Li 2006
Illustrations copyright © Mike Phillips 2006

1 3 5 7 9 8 6 4 2

A CIP catalogue record for this book is available from
the British Library.

Design by John Fordham

Printed and bound in China

Picture credits:
Science Museum/Science and Society Picture Library
Pages 1, 3, 7, 8, 9 (top and bottom), 11 (top and bottom),
12, 13, 14, 15, 17 (top and bottom), 19 (all), 23, 30.
Mary Evans Picture Library Page 21.
Getty Page 26.

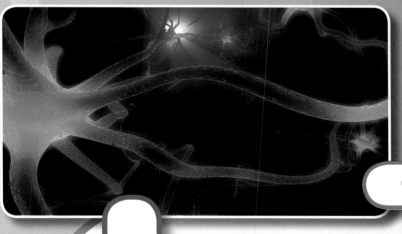

CONTENTS

science
museum

SO YOU WANT TO BE A SURGEON?

The work of a surgeon sounds like a job description for a superhero. There are challenges to overcome, sudden emergencies to deal with, nail-biting moments and even chances to save people's lives. Working in the medical profession is certainly an exciting job, but it's also very hard work, involving studying for years, taking lots of exams and working long hours. But ultimately the surgeon's job has to be one of the toughest and most exciting in the world.

About six million operations are performed every year in England alone – that's a lot of surgeons working to improve the quality of people's lives. Do you think you might have what it takes? You'll need:

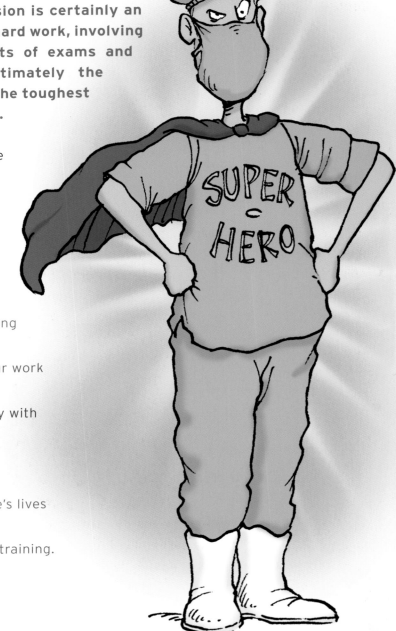

- **Stamina** – the ability to keep going even when you're tired
- **Motivation** – enthusiasm for your work and to keep learning new things
- **Compassion** – dealing sensitively with someone who is upset or scared
- **Ability to get on with people** – surgeons work as part of a team
- **Sense of responsibility** – people's lives are in your hands
- **Commitment** – it takes years of training.

BLOOD, PUKE … AND WORSE

It's also crucial that you're able to cope with the 'messy' side of medicine. If you're **squeamish** – the kind of person who can't stand the sight of blood or operations on TV – then a surgeon's life is probably not for you!

Up the medical ladder

Think you fit the bill? Then start by working as hard as you can at school, because you'll need A levels in science subjects to get into **medical school**. Here you'll spend five years studying for a degree, some of which will be spent learning about anatomy (structure of the body), pharmacology (the science of medical drugs), physiology (how the body works) and other aspects of medicine.

You'll also train at a hospital, working in groups led by experienced doctors. You could get the chance to study in a hospital abroad. Throughout the years of training there will be lots of exams that you will need to pass. Are you ready?

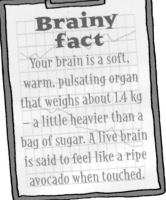

Brainy fact

Your brain is a soft, warm, pulsating organ that weighs about 1.4 kg – a little heavier than a bag of sugar. A live brain is said to feel like a ripe avocado when touched.

Specialist registrar (SpR) – 5 to 6 years

You will now have specialist training in your chosen surgical field, for example, neurosurgery (brain surgery), plastic surgery or paediatric surgery (children). If you're successful you will eventually become a **consultant** (top) **surgeon**. Congratulations!

Senior house officer (SHO) – 2 years

You will have decided on your **speciality** by now e.g. renal (kidney) or cardio (heart). Would-be surgeons undergo two years of surgical training.

Foundation course ('house job') – 2 years

All junior doctors are put on **placements** in a variety of different areas such as Accident and Emergency, Surgery and General Practice.

If you pass your exams and get your **degree**, you'll go on to what's called a 'house job' – working as part of a hospital team to learn more about patients and how to treat them.

START

THE REAL LIFE OF A BRAIN SURGEON

The job of a brain surgeon – or to use its proper medical name, **neurosurgeon** – is one of the most challenging and respected in any profession.

Neurosurgery is the area of medical science that deals with the **nervous system**. This includes the brain, spinal cord and the **nerves**.

THE BRAIN AND SPINAL CORD FORM THE **CENTRAL NERVOUS SYSTEM**. THEY RECEIVE INFORMATION SENT BY THE NERVES FROM YOUR BODY PARTS AND SEND INSTRUCTIONS OUT. FOR EXAMPLE, IF YOU TOUCH SOMETHING VERY HOT, YOUR NERVES 'TELL' YOUR BRAIN THAT IT'S HOT. YOUR BRAIN INSTRUCTS YOU TO TAKE YOUR HAND AWAY FROM THE HEAT.

THE NETWORK OF NERVES INSIDE YOUR BODY IS CALLED THE **PERIPHERAL NERVOUS SYSTEM**.

BRAIN

SPINAL CORD

NERVES

Brainy fact
Your brain is pink in colour because of all the blood flowing through it. One litre of blood flows through your brain every minute.

WHAT'S IT LIKE TO TRAIN AS A NEUROSURGEON?

Will is currently in the early stages of surgical training. He is working as a senior house officer in a hospital neurosurgery department.

Why did you decide to specialize in neurosurgery?
I'm fascinated by the way the brain works and by how diseases of the central nervous system affect people, their behaviour and actions. It's also interesting to look at scans of brains and spinal columns.

What are the best and worst aspects of the job?
Making sick people better is obviously very rewarding. It's also exciting, as every day something unexpected happens and there are often emergencies to deal with. The worst parts are the long hours and the huge responsibility – making decisions that may have life or death consequences for the patient. It can be emotionally draining, as well as physically demanding.

When was the first time you saw a real brain?
As a medical student I dissected a real brain. It was soft, like putting a knife through butter. I haven't yet cut into a live brain, but the big difference is that a live brain constantly pulsates.

Wax model of a human brain

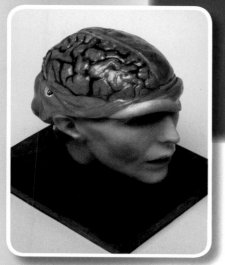

Have you performed a brain operation yet?
I have assisted in several operations – all were incredibly tense and exciting. Sometimes the patient is actually awake and talking to the surgeon while he or she is operating on them! It's awe-inspiring to actually see the brain and think that it houses all your thoughts and feelings.

A day in the life of a surgeon

Most neurosurgeons have lists of operations to perform on two days a week. Another day (and night) is spent 'on call' – dealing with emergency cases that may suddenly come in. The rest of the week is spent visiting patients on the wards, teaching students, writing reports and organizing budgets, among other things. There's also research to do – in the medical profession you never stop learning and trying to discover new things.

THE VERY FIRST 'SURGEONS'

If you decide to train as a surgeon you will become part of a long and fascinating tradition that dates all the way back to prehistoric times.

A hole in the head

The earliest evidence of 'surgery' has been found on ancient human skulls, some of which date back 10,000 years. These show that the skulls' owners had once undergone an operation called **trepanning** – cutting a hole through a skull while the person was alive. It must have been a painful and dangerous procedure, particularly as they did not have anaesthetics (painkillers). A sharpened edge of a stone or flint would have been used to make the hole.

Why did they do it?

No one is sure, but we know that ideas about medicine were very different then. People may have thought that illness was caused by evil spirits, and that a hole in the head would allow the spirits to escape. Or they may have been trying to improve their health in some way, perhaps thinking that making a hole would relieve the pressure of headaches.

Trepanned skulls have been found all over the world, often along with the piece of bone that had been cut out of the skull.

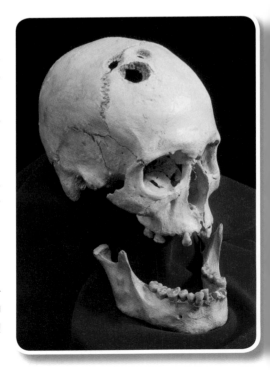

This skull was found in Palestine and is about 4,000 years old. It has four trepanned holes – but amazingly the person survived the process, as the bone shows signs of healing!

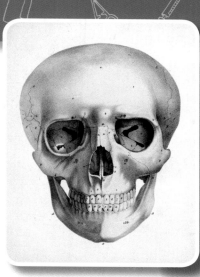

Illustration of the human skull by the French anatomist and surgeon **Jules Cloquet** (1815–1859)

THE SKULL

Your skull is formed by two sets of bones – the bones of your face and the bones of your **cranium**, which make up your forehead and the back of your head. There are 28 bones altogether.

- The cranium is a large bony case that protects the brain from damage. It is made up of eight flat bones and is about half a centimetre thick.

- The bottom of the skull has an opening where your spinal cord connects to your brain.

Modern-day trepanning

As a brain surgeon, many of your operations will involve cutting through the skull in order to reach the brain. The surgeon uses a small electric saw to cut the hole, being very careful not to press too hard. Underneath is a 1 mm-thick membrane called the **meninges**, that covers the pulsating brain. This must also be gently cut. The patient is anaesthetized and doesn't feel a thing.

Ancient surgeries

Trepanning isn't the only example of early surgery:

- **The Mesopotamians** (4000 – 3500 BC) used instruments called lancets to make cuts and perform operations on the eyes. One of their kings, Hammurabi, set down guidelines to govern this surgery. One of them read:

  'If a physician performs an operation on a commoner's slave with a bronze lancet [sharp tool] and causes his death, he shall make good slave for slave…'

- An ancient Hindu doctor called **Susruta** (around 1500 BC) could perform a type of plastic surgery. He was able to replace an organ such as the nose with skin cut from another part of the patient's body.

Brainy fact

The ancient Egyptians designed special tools to remove the brain from the skull when preparing bodies to be mummified.

An antique trepan or crown saw used for perforating the skull

MEDICINE MOVES ON

Stitching up the wounds of mauled and perforated gladiators and extracting arrows from injured soldiers were routine tasks for a surgeon in the times of the ancient Greeks and Romans. These were exciting times for doctors – and several became famous for their new and sophisticated ideas about health and medicine.

Greek doctors

Ancient Greek doctors were once thought to be the best in the world. One of the most famous was the philosopher **Hippocrates** (460–370 BC), who is described as the 'father of medicine'. He took away much of the superstition that surrounded medicine and focused instead on the physical causes of illnesses and injuries.

Like Hippocrates, **Aristotle** (384–322 BC) believed that proper medical investigation was the only way to make progress in medicine. He was one of the first doctors to actually dissect a dead human body.

Galen – the most famous Roman physician

Galen (AD 129–199) also believed that observation was the way forward and he made impressive advances in anatomy. He learned a great deal about the human body from working as a doctor to the Roman gladiators, describing their wounds as 'windows to the body', but he never once dissected a real human. Because his knowledge of internal organs came from animals, mostly pigs and monkeys, he did get some things wrong.

Brainy fact

Galen made the first proper studies of the nervous system, brain and heart, and his work was the basis of medicine for the next 1,500 years.

THE CUTTING EDGE

Dissection is the process of separating or cutting something into pieces.

As a medical student today you will probably be asked to dissect a human body as this is thought to be a very effective way of learning about how they work and are put together. However, in most early cultures, dissection was forbidden.

Attitudes began to change in the time of the ancient Greeks, when philosophers decided that the body and the soul were completely separate from each other. Physicians such as Aristotle began to dissect human bodies and make valuable discoveries about our anatomy. But during the time of the Romans dissection was banned again. This is why Galen could use only animals for his research.

Three pairs of Roman surgical shears AD 200–500

Greek and Roman surgery

We know that Greek and Roman surgeons had plenty of surgical instruments to choose from, as more than a hundred different types were found in the ruins of Roman Pompeii, a city destroyed by a volcanic eruption in AD 79. They include:

Replicas of Roman surgical instruments found at Pompeii

- **Scalpel** – with a steel blade for slicing through flesh

- **Forceps** (a pincer-like instrument) – for removing objects such as bone fragments

- Small **hand saw** – for cutting through flesh and bone, used for amputations (removal of limbs).

Most surgery took place on the external parts of the body. This would have included lancing abcesses, stitching together the edges of wounds after battle and removing infected teeth. Trepanning skulls was also a common procedure.

SAVING THE ANCIENTS

Modern-day surgeons can perform incredible life-saving operations because they have the benefit of knowledge that has been handed down to them through hundreds of years of medical learning. But nearly all the knowledge that the Greeks and Romans had gained was lost in the third century AD, when the Roman Empire collapsed. The Dark Ages descended upon Europe.

For hundreds of years after the Romans fell, the **Arab world** led the way in science and medicine. Arab scholars collected ancient manuscripts and books from the Western world containing the ideas of famed physicians such as Hippocrates. They translated them into Arabic and Persian. These texts were then handed down to later generations.

Persian surgical-instrument set

The Muslim law of the Arab world did not allow dissection, so most of their knowledge of the human body came from Galen, whose discoveries – and, indeed, many inaccuracies – were passed on.

Arab achievements

- The Arabs were renowned for their advances in **pharmacology** – the science of drugs, including their uses and effects – and their doctors became highly skilled at making medicines. The huge Arabian city of Baghdad housed the first pharmacies in the world.

- The Arabs were the first to use **alcohol** to clean wounds, which proved very effective against infection, as it kills bacteria (germs).

- The Arab world was famous for its great **hospitals**, which had advanced facilities such as medical and surgical wards, operating theatres and pharmacies. Hospitals were built in all parts of the Islamic Empire – during Arab rule in Spain, 52 were built in the city of Cordoba alone.

This reconstruction at the Science Museum shows a cataract operation in Persia, around AD 1000. The surgeon is pushing a needle into the patient's eye to push aside the clouded lens.

Surgery

Arab doctors performed many different surgical operations, including the removal of varicose veins, kidney stones and the re-setting of dislocated limbs. **Al-Zahrawi** (AD 936–1013) was the most famous surgeon of this period. He wrote a manual on surgery called *Al-Tasrif*, illustrated with drawings of about one hundred surgical instruments.

Some other interesting surgical advances were made during this time:

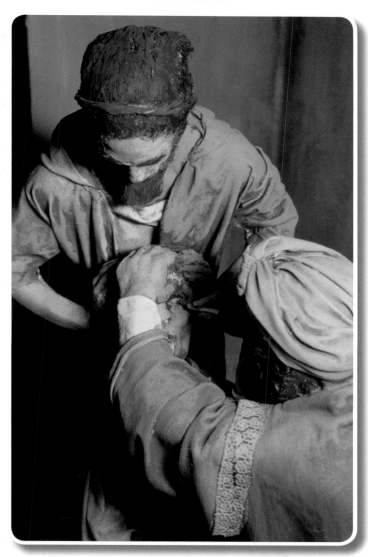

- **Cataract surgery** – doctors could remove cataracts (clouding of the lens) from an eye, enabling the patient to see again.

- **Cauterization** – this involved using a hot instrument to burn or sear wounds, sealing blood vessels during an operation.

- **Early anaesthetics** – sponges soaked in narcotic (sleep-inducing) drugs were placed over the patient's face during surgery to lessen the pain.

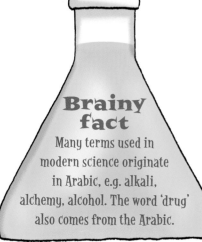

Brainy fact
Many terms used in modern science originate in Arabic, e.g. alkali, alchemy, alcohol. The word 'drug' also comes from the Arabic.

ANATOMICAL WONDERS

As a student doctor you will spend a great deal of time studying the intricate workings of the human body. But it wasn't always like this. How did students hundreds of years ago get their information?

A new beginning

No medical advances were made in Europe during the Dark Ages and people went back to the old superstitious ways of thinking, believing that illness was caused by evil forces or that it was a punishment from God. But in the late 14th century a new interest in learning and knowledge came about, which lasted for about 200 years. This was known as the **Renaissance** (meaning 'rebirth').

Vesalius – the great anatomist

The Renaissance first began in Italy, the home of **Andreas Vesalius** (1514–64), a doctor who later became a professor at the University of Padua. Vesalius became famous for his dissections, because they were unlike other lectures at that time.

The old ways

Students had learned by watching a person called a **barber-surgeon** (who was not a trained doctor) dissecting animals. They used Galen's works for reference and believed everything in them was true.

Vesalius changed everything. He performed dissections himself and relied on his own observations rather than Galen's. In 1539 a judge allowed Vesalius to dissect **human bodies** for the first time – the corpses of executed criminals. Vesalius commissioned artists to make incredibly detailed drawings of his findings, the first really accurate diagrams of the human body to be produced. These marked the beginning of scientific anatomy.

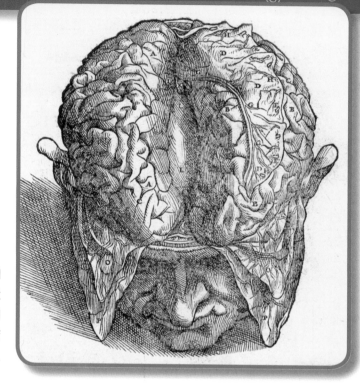

This diagram commissioned by Vesalius was the most detailed study that had ever been made of the brain at that time.

Vesalius's famous book of drawings, **De Humani Corporis Fabrica** (On the Structure of the Human Body), was published in 1543, but many of the illustrations were different from Galen's. People couldn't believe that Galen could ever have been wrong and, at first, found it very hard to accept Vesalius's work.

Modern-day learning

Groups of medical students are introduced to their 'body' at the beginning of the year. This is a person who has requested that their body be used for medical research when they die. Each group of students will gradually dissect the body, part by part throughout the year. At each session, the professor of surgery or anatomy demonstrator will first show them how to dissect a particular organ before the students practise themselves. Books are also studied, including the famous **Gray's Anatomy**. At the end of the year the students may be invited to the cremation of the person they have been dissecting.

BARBAROUS PRACTICES

Surgeons are highly respected people these days, but this wasn't always the case. In fact, the surgeon's job actually sprang from the profession of barbering – cutting hair.

From barber to surgeon

It's strange to think that a barber could ever have done the job of a surgeon, but that's exactly what used to happen. Early doctors avoided doing surgery and preferred to leave what was seen as a lowly job to the unskilled barbers, who used razors and other instruments to perform amputations, extract teeth and carry out a grisly procedure called bloodletting. These '**barber-surgeons**' formed their own organization in 1096, but it took many years for surgery to become a respected profession. During the Renaissance a French barber-surgeon called **Ambroise Paré** (1510–1590) did much to help surgery's reputation and he is now called the 'father of surgery', not to be confused with Hippocrates (see page 10), the 'father of medicine'.

(see page 10)

In fact, surgeons were not formally distinct from barbers in England until 1745, when a law was passed separating the two professions. The surgeons went on to form their own organization and the job gradually developed into the highly skilled profession it is today. **The Royal College of Surgeons** was founded in 1800.

Haircuts
Shaves
Blood-
letting
Amputations
Teeth pulled

Brainy fact

Bloodletting often caused people to faint or swoon through loss of blood, but this was regarded as quite normal.

A leech jar, two bleeding bowls and four lancets used for bloodletting in the 18th century

Bloodletting

Bloodletting was a gruesome-sounding but very common procedure that took place from ancient times right up to the 19th century. It originated from the ancient Greek idea that disease could be cured by restoring 'balance' to the body. They believed that blood was one of the substances (or 'humours') that needed to be controlled, and this idea continued for hundreds of years. Over the years different methods were used to release blood from the body, including:

- cutting open the veins with a sharp implement to let the blood drain out

- placing live blood-sucking leeches on various parts of the body

- putting heated cups over small cuts on the skin. As the air in the cups cools down, blood is drawn out from the cuts. This practise still exists today.

That innocent-looking red and white striped pole that can be seen outside traditional barbers' shops is actually a symbol of bloodletting. The patient would hold very tightly to a rod, to make the veins on their arms stand out. Then the barber would cut open the veins, letting blood flow out. The striped pole represents the rod, the red and white stripes symbolize both the blood-soaked and clean bandages.

A 'mechanical leech' set, c.1850

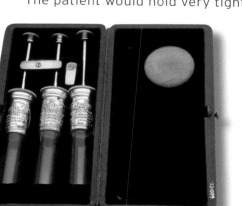

SCARY SURGERY

For hundreds of years, having an operation was likely to be a painful and dangerous experience. Little was known about the importance of hygiene, and patients often developed serious infections after surgery. Many died as a result.

How to be a surgeon in the Middle Ages

You are an apprentice barber-surgeon in 1450. Watch and learn as your master performs a common operation – amputation (removal of a limb).

1. Your patient is a young man who has fallen off a cart, crushing his leg under the wheel. It needs to be amputated before gangrene sets in.

2. The operation must be done as quickly as possible because it will be extremely painful. Some patients have even been known to jump off the operating table and run away during surgery!

3. The only thing you have to dull the pain is alcohol – give the patient some wine or brandy to drink and that might help a little.

4. Now tie cords tightly around the patient's leg to stop it bleeding too much when we start cutting.

5. Hold the patient down while we saw the leg off as quickly as possible. Try to ignore his screams. Once it's done, pour wine over the wound and stitch it up.

Brainy fact

Napoleon's war surgeon, Dominique-Jean Larrey (1766–1842), described amputations where three men were needed to hold the patient down during the operation.

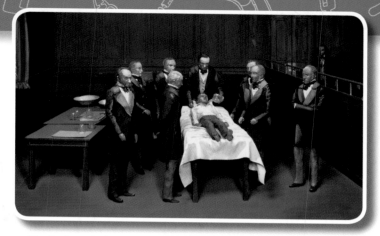

These days – luckily for us – having surgery is no longer the stuff of nightmares. Patients don't need to suffer unnecessary pain and they have an excellent chance of survival. This is partly due to some major discoveries that were made in the 19th century.

The first surgical operation carried out with a general anaesthetic took place in Boston, USA, in 1846.

- In 1846 a substance called **ether** was given to a patient who was about to undergo an amputation. He fell unconscious, remained so throughout and felt no pain. Another substance, **chloroform**, was also found to have a similar effect, as was a gas called **nitrous oxide** (known as laughing gas), which had been discovered many years before, but had not been widely used. The use of these early **anaesthetics** meant that internal organs of the body could now be operated on as patients could bear to have surgeons spending longer at their work.

Chloroform drop bottles. Chloroform is actually a poison and was dangerous to use.

- A French chemist called **Louis Pasteur** discovered that harmful bacteria were carried in the air. This led to the development of **antiseptics** – substances that kill disease-causing bacteria; 'anti' = against, 'septic' = infection. These have been used in surgery ever since to kill the germs that cause infections. Before this time no one had realized that there were tiny micro-organisms on the surgical instruments and even on the hands of the surgeon.

- A surgeon called **Joseph Lister**, hearing about this discovery, began washing his hands and instruments thoroughly with carbolic acid (a liquid with antiseptic properties). This technique was gradually adopted by other surgeons and soon saved many patients' lives.

CORPSES AND CADAVERS

From the early 1800s onwards, the desire to learn more about medical matters grew and so did the number of medical students. The establishment of medical schools also created an entirely new market – for dead human bodies (called corpses or cadavers).

The rise of the bodysnatchers

The law allowed only the bodies of executed criminals to be used for dissection. Unfortunately there just weren't enough to go round, and the demand led to an unpleasant new phenomenon – **grave robbing**. Because the medical schools paid for bodies, some people saw this as a money-making opportunity. They visited graveyards at night, dug up recently buried bodies and sold them to the colleges, who did not ask where the bodies had come from.

Medicine in Edinburgh

Bodysnatching was particularly rife in Edinburgh, where the Faculty of Medicine became one of the most highly respected centres of learning in Europe by the mid-18th century. Students could learn about medicine or surgery at the university and its teaching hospital. The surgeons of Edinburgh could trace their origins back to 1505, when the first group of barber-surgeons was properly recognized in the city.

From snatching – to murder

William Burke and **William Hare** were Irish labourers who lived in 19th-century Edinburgh. They made money from robbing graves at night, but they didn't stop at that. Burke and Hare decided to murder people too, selling the bodies to the medical school. They were finally caught, but not before they had killed 16 people in just under a year.

Brainy fact

Researchers at the University of Nottingham have developed a virtual-reality brain-surgery simulator. The trainee surgeon can practise brain surgery in the same way as you can play a computer game.

Virtual reality bodies?

Things have changed a lot since the days when medical schools were so desperate for bodies that they would ask no questions of the dubious people who provided them. Today's medical students learn from the bodies of people who have donated them for research. Computers are increasingly being used as a teaching aid, along with software that provides accurate visual simulations of the human body. And there may come a time in the future when trainee doctors and surgeons have access to even more exciting technology. One idea is to create a computerized '**virtual patient**', which would enable a student to perform a realistic three-dimensional dissection, digitally 'slicing' away skin, muscle and bone. Virtual reality could also have many other applications for the medical world and may one day revolutionize surgery.

WAR WOUNDS

As a surgeon in the future, you will hopefully never need to operate on a wounded soldier during a war. But in the past, doctors and surgeons have had to treat injured soldiers coming from the battlefields in the most terrible circumstances. However, huge advances in knowledge and techniques have been made during times of war.

The First World War 1914–1918

Being a surgeon during the First World War must have been an extremely challenging and difficult job:

- This was the first major war in which modern weapons, such as machine guns and explosive shells, were used. They caused devastating injuries.

- There were huge numbers of wounded soldiers and many different kinds of injuries to attend to, such as gunshot wounds, shrapnel injuries and burns. Shrapnel is the name for fragments and other objects thrown out at high speed by an exploding object, such as a bomb.

Many of the casualties had severe head and facial wounds, and war surgeons had to quickly develop new techniques in plastic surgery in order to operate on injuries such as shattered jaws and blown-off noses. A special surgical treatment centre was set up in France, where much of the fighting took place.

WHAT IS PLASTIC SURGERY?

There is no actual plastic used in this kind of surgery. The name comes from the ancient Greek word 'plastikos', which means to mould or give form. Plastic surgeons mould or reconstruct parts of the body. To do this, they often use skin grafts – taking skin from one part of the body to replace damaged or lost skin elsewhere.

The idea goes as far back as 4,000 years, when the first skin grafts were performed by the ancient Indian physician, **Susruta**.

Alexander Fleming (1881–1955) in his laboratory. The petrie dishes on the desk contain penicillin mould.

By the time of the **Second World War** (1939–1945) plastic surgery had progressed even further and surgeons successfully operated on many injured soldiers, sailors and airmen. Other medical advances also helped save lives. **X-rays** (first discovered in 1895) were now being used to help doctors see exactly where bullets and shrapnel had lodged in the body. And the use of a new drug – an **antibiotic** – meant that there were far fewer deaths and amputations from infected wounds during the Second World War.

Amazing antibiotics

In 1928, a scientist called **Alexander Fleming** discovered by accident that the mould **penicillin** could kill or slow down the growth of bacteria. This first antibiotic was developed some years later and used during the Second World War. It was nicknamed the 'wonder drug' because of its effectiveness against certain types of infection. Antibiotics have been a major breakthrough for modern medicine.

BACK TO THE BRAIN

Trainee surgeons who decide to specialize in neurosurgery do so because they are fascinated by the human brain. And no wonder. The brain is the most amazing and complex organ in the human body.

You and your brain

Your brain is the place that contains your thoughts, memories, dreams and experiences — the things that make you a unique person. Without your brain, you wouldn't be able to have feelings and emotions. You couldn't think, speak or move. It's the control centre of the body.

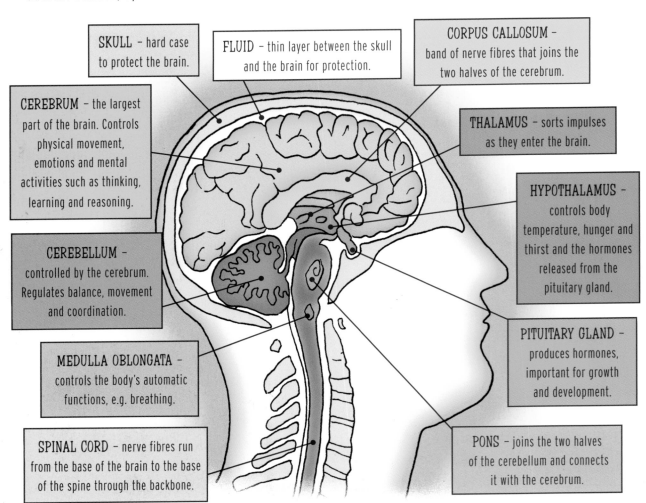

SKULL – hard case to protect the brain.

FLUID – thin layer between the skull and the brain for protection.

CORPUS CALLOSUM – band of nerve fibres that joins the two halves of the cerebrum.

CEREBRUM – the largest part of the brain. Controls physical movement, emotions and mental activities such as thinking, learning and reasoning.

THALAMUS – sorts impulses as they enter the brain.

HYPOTHALAMUS – controls body temperature, hunger and thirst and the hormones released from the pituitary gland.

CEREBELLUM – controlled by the cerebrum. Regulates balance, movement and coordination.

MEDULLA OBLONGATA – controls the body's automatic functions, e.g. breathing.

PITUITARY GLAND – produces hormones, important for growth and development.

SPINAL CORD – nerve fibres run from the base of the brain to the base of the spine through the backbone.

PONS – joins the two halves of the cerebellum and connects it with the cerebrum.

Inside the brain

As you know, the brain, the spinal cord and the nerves are connected and, together, form your nervous system. Information travels from the nerves around the body to the brain.

- The **cerebrum** has a soft bumpy texture and looks rather like a giant walnut. It is divided into two halves or **hemispheres**.

- The right hemisphere controls muscles in the left side of the body, and the left hemisphere controls muscles in the right side.

- The cerebrum does many different jobs. It has an area that picks up information from sense organs, such as the eyes, ears and nose. Another area uses the information to make decisions, and a third area sends impulses and instructions out to muscles and glands.

Brainy fact

Your brain is currently receiving about 100 million pieces of information, which are being sent to your nervous system by your ears, eyes, nose, tongue and touch sensors.

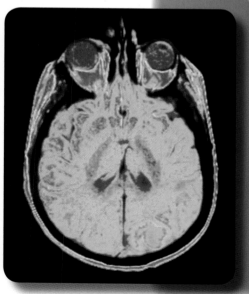

MRI (Magnetic Resonance Imaging) scan showing a brain tumour (pale blue at the bottom right)

NEW WAYS OF SEEING

The invention of sophisticated imaging techniques has enabled scientists to 'see' inside the living brain and to discover some of its functions:

- **MRI scan (Magnetic Resonance Imaging)** – uses strong magnetic power to produce scans of internal body parts. MRI allows us to see which parts of the brain are active when different tasks are performed.

- **CT scan (Computerized Tomography)** – X-ray beams are used to view 'slices' of a body part, which are reassembled by computer to produce a detailed image.

- **PET scan (Positron Emission Tomography)** – uses nuclear technology to produce a three-dimensional image that can show functions such as blood flow. This information can tell us how much activity is going on in each part of the brain.

After years spent studying to be a neurosurgeon you might think that you'd know everything possible about the brain. But you'd be wrong. There are many areas of the brain that are still a mystery to science.

Tiny messengers

We know that the brain and the rest of the nervous system are made up of billions of cells called **neurons**. These are specialized nerve cells that are in constant communication with each other. 'Messages' are sent across tiny gaps (synapses) between each neuron by chemical messengers called **neurotransmitters**.

Neurons work by processing information coming in or out of our nervous system, whether it relates to movement, to the senses or to thinking. Many different kinds of neuron are needed to cope with this huge amount of information – scientists think there are 10,000 different types.

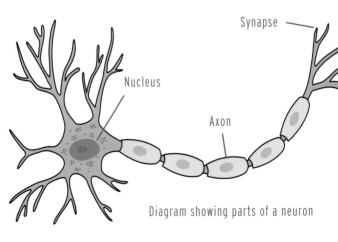

Synapse

Nucleus

Axon

Diagram showing parts of a neuron

INTO THE UNKNOWN

- It was only recently discovered that neurons can actually regenerate throughout a person's life. We used to think that only children and young adults could grow new brain cells and that once a neuron was killed off, it was gone forever. But research has shown us that new cells can grow in the **hippocampus**, the part of the brain that controls memory and learning.

Diagram showing the position of the hippocampus in the brain

- Scientists are also starting to think that the brain could be a bit like a muscle – the harder you use it, the more it grows. Exercising the brain by using it in stimulating ways may cause the neurons to branch and make more connections with other neurons. This means that even old people's brains may be able to change and adapt, having a better chance of staying healthy. It also offers new hope for preventing and treating brain diseases.

- No one has ever worked out exactly why the brain needs sleep or why we dream. We know that sleep plays an essential part in the development of the brain and that it seems to be important for memory and learning. Sleep may even help form our memories.

- Are you left- or right-handed? Whichever you are, scientists don't know the reason why. We know that each of the two hemispheres of the cerebrum controls the opposite side of the body. They also have different functions – the right is more important for emotion, recognizing faces and music, while the left is important for language, maths and reasoning. But we still don't know if there is a connection between the brain and right- or left-handedness.

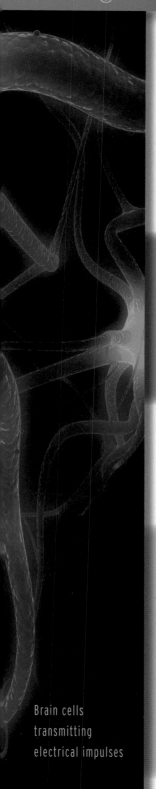

Brain cells transmitting electrical impulses

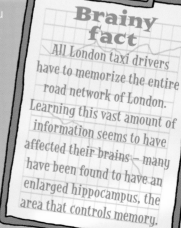

Brainy fact

All London taxi drivers have to memorize the entire road network of London. Learning this vast amount of information seems to have affected their brains – many have been found to have an enlarged hippocampus, the area that controls memory.

IN THE THEATRE

The big day has arrived. After all that hard work and study, you're ready to perform your first operation.

Today you'll be removing a blood clot from the brain of a person who has injured their head in an accident.

Getting ready

First you'll put on a gown, mask and rubber gloves, all of which have been treated with steam to kill any bacteria on them. You'll also change your germ-ridden outdoor shoes for plastic clogs and cover your hair with a cap.

Inside the operating theatre

Surgeons and their teams often like to have music playing while they work because it creates a relaxing atmosphere.

Asleep or awake?

In some brain operations, the patient stays fully awake. This lets the neurosurgeon know immediately if a function such as speech or motor function (the ability to use your muscles) is being affected. Instead of a general anaesthetic, which makes a person completely unconscious, the patient receives a local anaesthetic, which only numbs the part of the body being operated on. The brain itself does not feel pain, as it contains no pain-sensing nerves.

CLOCKS – There are two clocks on the wall. One displays the time and another lets the surgical team know the amount of time that has passed since the operation started.

X-RAY VIEWING SCREEN – The surgeon can look at the patient's X-rays for more information while he or she is doing the operation.

THE HEAD NEURO-SURGEON – He or she leads the team and performs the surgery. The consultant neurosurgeon usually knows about the patient and their history because he or she will have examined them at a clinic and visited them on the ward. In emergencies, however, there is little chance to do this.

SUCTION UNIT – This removes blood and any other excess fluids from the operation site.

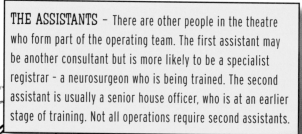

THE ASSISTANTS – There are other people in the theatre who form part of the operating team. The first assistant may be another consultant but is more likely to be a specialist registrar - a neurosurgeon who is being trained. The second assistant is usually a senior house officer, who is at an earlier stage of training. Not all operations require second assistants.

THE ANAESTHETIST – A highly trained doctor who specializes in the use of anaesthetic medicine and gases. If the patient needs a general anaesthetic they will give them an injection or gas to breathe in through a mask to make them unconscious. The anaesthetist will control the flow of gas using a special machine on a trolley.

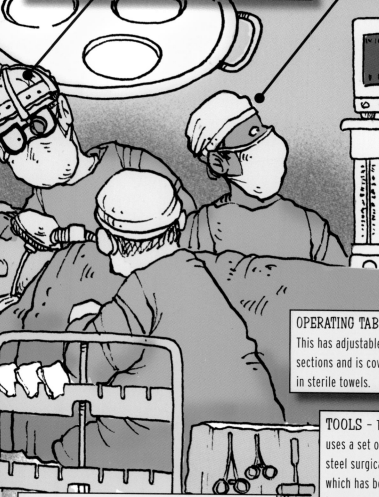

MONITORS – These machines display the patient's vital functions, such as heart rate and blood pressure. They are constantly checked.

OPERATING TABLE – This has adjustable sections and is covered in sterile towels.

TOOLS – The surgeon uses a set of stainless-steel surgical tools, which has been sterilized in a machine called an autoclave.

SWAB RACK – The number of swabs (pieces of material used for cleaning around the wound) used is recorded and they are counted before the operation is finished to make sure that none is left inside the body.

Brainy fact

Neurosurgery is an extremely delicate and precise procedure – a slip of just a millimetre could be very dangerous. Years of training help give neurosurgeons the skill and confidence they need to do the job.

SURGERY – THE FUTURE

Surgeons today have the knowledge and equipment to do incredible things, from slicing out brain tumours to transplanting faces. And there are more exciting new developments to come.

No more cuts?

For hundreds of years surgery has been performed in the same way. The surgeon makes a cut in the patient using a **scalpel** – a small and very sharp knife – then operates on the organs by hand, using metal instruments. But over the last twenty years another kind of surgery has been introduced, one where the patient does not need to be cut open. For example, modern **laser surgery** allows surgeons to use the power of a laser beam to slice through tissue or to remove abnormal cells. The patient recovers more quickly and can spend less time in hospital. More techniques like this are being developed all the time.

The invisible blade

Having to saw through the skull in neurosurgery is no longer necessary for certain operations. The '**X-knife**' is an instrument that uses highly focused beams of radiation, enabling brain surgery to be performed without cutting through or even entering the skull. The 'invisible blade' can remove brain tumours, even ones that are too deep for normal surgery to reach. Patients can be awake while their brains are being operated on, allowing the surgeon to know instantly what effect the surgery is having!

One-stop surgery

Some scientists believe that one day a simple visit to the doctor will replace the nerve-racking experience of going into the operating theatre. For example, high-tech imaging systems could identify cancerous cells in the body, then treat them immediately with laser beams or X-rays – all under one roof.

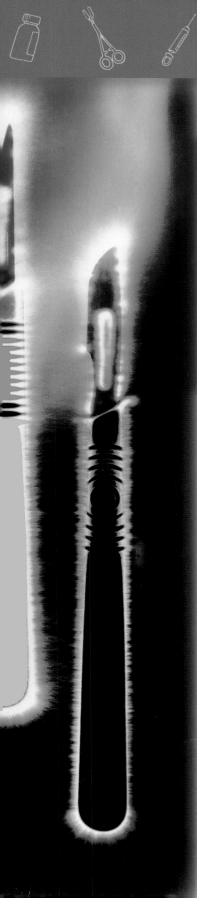

Other new ideas replace people with artificial humans:

The robot surgeon

How would you feel about being operated on by a robot? It may sound like a scene from science fiction, but it's already happening. A robotic arm has been developed that allows surgery to be performed remotely – meaning the surgeon can operate without having to be anywhere near the patient. The surgeon controls the robotic arm with the use of a computer, helped by images from a video monitor and an MRI scanner. Surgeons in the USA have already successfully used computers and robots to take part in operations in Italy. One of the advantages of the robot surgeon is that it never suffers from shaky hands!

The virtual patient

Surgeons may soon be able to practise on a patient as many times as they like. CT and MRI scans from the patient's body could be used to create an incredibly realistic 'virtual-reality' display of the patient's organs. The surgeon can then perform the operation 'virtually', getting the procedure just right before attempting the real thing.

Brainy fact

A new brain scanner has recently been developed that uses beams of light to scan newborn babies' brains, helping to identify which babies are at risk of brain damage.

So if you want a job that's incredibly challenging, helps people and uses the very latest cutting-edge technology, neurosurgery could be just the thing for you.

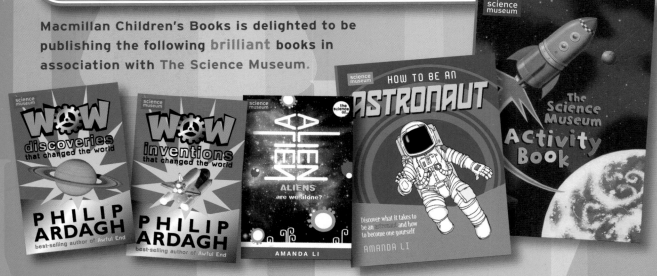